Michael Hale

January 2022

**DO NOT REMOVE
CARDS FROM POCKET**

ACPL Discard

ALLEN COUNTY PUBLIC LIBRARY

FORT WAYNE, INDIANA 46802

You may return this book to any agency, branch,
or bookmobile of the Allen County Public Library.

"Good golly, Miss Molly,
has America always
been like this?"

Z. de Tocqueville

QUOTE, UNQUOTE

JONATHAN WILLIAMS

ILLUSTRATIONS BY
GLEN BAXTER

TEN SPEED PRESS
Berkeley, California

The author wishes to thank Jordan Davies, of New
York City, who published the first five sections of this
work in an edition of 100 copies in 1983. And
Jonathan Greene, of *Gnomon Books*, Frankfort,
Kentucky, who reprinted this and added section six in
an edition of 1500 copies in 1985. Both books were
entitled IN THE AZURE OVER THE
SQUALOR, which may explain why only the 83
faithful and the wandering delusional ever bought
them.

    J. W.

1☉
TEN SPEED PRESS
P.O. Box 7123
Berkeley, California 94707

Author photo by Guy Mendes
Folk art in author photo by James Harold Jennings,
Stoakes County, NC
Book Design by Nancy Austin
Cover Art and Illustration by Glen Baxter
Typesetting by Wilsted & Taylor

Library of Congress Catalog Card Number: *88-05180*
ISBN 0-89815-302-6

Printed in the United States of America

1   2   3   4   5   6—93   92   91   90   89

☒ A Note to this Edition

About half of what follows was stylishly published a few years ago by *Gnomon Press*, the excellent (but indeed underground) small press operated by the poet Jonathan Greene at one of America's best and most covert addresses: O'nan's Bend Road, Bagdad, Kentucky. The world beats not a path to J. Greene's hospitable door in the woods, but Phil Wood and George Young, the canny gents at *Ten Speed Press*, think there may actually be a market for these findings of mine in our miraculous country, where people like Sparky Anderson and Dan Quayle say the oddest things.

There have been writers from Heraklitos ("the road up is the road down") to Stravinsky ("Wagner is the Puccini of music!") to remind us of the play of the mind in the language and the sight of the imagination in full flower. I am an insatiable collector of such petalled wit, wisdom, absurdity, and insolence. It is to be found primarily in texts, but also in good conversation, in simply passing through a literate world. A writer regards words with the same passion as collectors of arrowheads, amethyst crystals, galax leaves, and birdsong.

A gift of this book to any unabashed boy or girl might save a doting parent $75,000 in costs at some loathsome brain factory for the mindless and overly ambitious. People who like this book often buy it ten copies at a time. It is a caviar, grand-cru alternative, in its way, to *White Trash Cooking*, Ernest Matthew Mickler's triumphant essay in rampant democracy.

The Decline of the West may have declined indeed, but, Herr Spengler, *now* is where we live and breathe. As Sparky says "What was was was! What is is is!" Breathe deeply. The lines are still fresh.

Jonathan Williams
Highlands, North Carolina
October 26, 1988

I

Aesthetics is for the Artists like Ornithology is for the Birds.

Barnett Newman

Responsibility is to keep the ability to respond.

Robert Duncan

Great things are done when men and
   mountains meet;
this is not done by Jostling in the Street.

William Blake

Now I am ice; now I am sorrel.

Henry David Thoreau

I am that he whose brains are scattered endlessly.

William Carlos Williams

Do not spoil your nature. But don't ask me what nature is either. There are supposed to be above 200 definitions of it — one is good enough for me.

Edward Dahlberg

I do the very best I know how — the very best I can; and I mean to keep doing so until the end. If the end brings me out all right, what is said against me won't amount to anything. If the end brings me out wrong, ten angels swearing I was right would make no difference.

Abraham Lincoln

Stand up and use your ears like a man!

Charles Ives

The poet is the man who puts things together.

R. Buckminster Fuller

A pine tree is not an oak tree.

Louis Sullivan

Ja wohl, mein nomme is not Anton Bruckner.

Erik Alfred Leslie Satie

I don't know
what the Left is doing,
said the Right Hand,
but it looks fascinating.

James Broughton

We may eventually come to realize that
Chastity is no more a virtue than
Malnutrition.

Alex Comfort

They ought to tear you down and put up a
new building!

Groucho Marx

90 percent of the worst human beings I know
are poets. Most poets these days are so
square they have to walk around the block
just to turn over in bed.

Kenneth Rexroth

The food of the soul is Light and Space.

Herman Melville

The song is heat!
Charles Olson

Craft is perfected attention.
Robert Kelly

To write a symphony means to me to
construct a world with all the tools of the
available technique. The ever new and
changing content determines its own form.
Gustav Mahler

The time will come when a single original
carrot will be pregnant with revolution.
Paul Cézanne

You can't derail a train by standing directly
in front of it, or, not quite. But, a tiny piece
of steel, properly placed . . .
Robert Creeley

Dig and sow!
Abbot Luan

Nature & Art in this together Suit:
What is Most Grand is always most Minute.
William Blake

The poet, no less than the scientist, works on
the assumption that inert and live things and
relations hold enough interest to keep him
alive as part of nature.
Louis Zukofsky

All I ever did was make a little noise for
some guys that nobody was listening to.
Ezra Pound (in conversation, Venice, 1966)

The world is full of strangers,
they are very strange;
and I shall never meet them —
it is easy to arrange.
Florine Stettheimer

Odi et amo!
Catullus

Whether it is fun to go to bed with a good book depends a great deal on who's reading it.

Kenneth Patchen

DEGAS: Voilà, I've got this great idea for a poem!

MALLARMÉ: Hélas, mon ami, poems are made out of words, not ideas.

Just get the right syllable in the proper place.

Jonathan Swift

QUESTIONER: If you had your life to live over, what would you do differently?

W. C. FIELDS: I'd live over a saloon.

More light!

Goethe

What is the answer . . . ? What was the question?

Gertrude Stein (last words)

If you don't know, why ask?
  John Cage

To live is to defend a form.
  Anton Webern

Madame, may I ask of what else should
Miss Sitwell's poems consist but 'words,
words, words'—dead larks, tea cozies,
antimacassars, and fragments of a stage
elephant????
  Osbert Sitwell

What to such as you anyhow such a poet as I?
  therefore leave my works
And go lull yourself with what you can
  understand, and with piano-tunes,
For I lull nobody, and you will never
  understand me.
  Walt Whitman

Music is to make people happy.
  Willie 'Bunk' Johnson

He speaks stones (so said Agrippa) and let his readers beware lest he break their heads.

Robert Burton

II

You can always tell white trash, but you can't tell it much.

Alvin Doyle Moore

Of course, literati are almost in every sense nastier than peasants.

Martin Seymour-Smith

None of us is/are entirely pleasant.

Robert Duncan

My neighbors down here in Barbour County, Alabama are kindly, intelligent, educated, and refined.

George Wallace

There are many things in this world.

Abraham Klax-Williams

I piss on it all — from a considerable height.

Céline

New Orleans sticks close to the Scriptures:
cry after Birth, rejoice after Death.
> *Ferdinand 'Jelly Roll' Morton*

May you always live in interesting times.
> *Ancient Chinese Curse*

Nicolai Vasilievich Gogol suffered from an
unfortunate love affair in extreme youth,
after which he took to unremitting
masturbation and eventually became a great
novelist.
> *Macy (from his* History of World
> Literature in One Volume*)*

Write! — if you find work.
> *Bob & Ray*

The poetic image, in its newness, opens a
future to language.
> *Gaston Bachelard*

Everything should be as simple as it is, but
not simpler.
> *Albert Einstein*

Anything simple always interests me.
David Hockney

I didn't need no diploma to do what I can do.
Louis 'Satchmo' Armstrong

The Goddess Fortune is the devil's servant,
ready to Kiss any one's Arse.
William Blake

Nothings lasts, neither Mr. Money nor Mrs.
Cunt.
Thomas Berger

I got them before they could get me.
*Vachel Lindsay (last words, after drinking
Lysol)*

For Christ's sake, can't you get them to turn
off the television!
Bob Brown (last words)

Books are out. Aquarius people like us don't have time anymore to read books.

Eryon Thomas (Dylan's daughter)

The proof of a poet is that his country absorbs him as affectionately as he has absorbed it.

Walt Whitman

I would almost say that my country is like a conquered province with foreign rulers, except that they are not foreigners and we are responsible for what they do.

Paul Goodman

Be present, be yourself. You are here. Objects are here. They are here for you only, because you see them.

Tibetan Lamaist Saying

The wogs begin at Calais!

The Sang-Froid Genius-Loci of Great Britain

I never hurt anybody but myself and that's
nobody's business but my own.
Billie Holiday

Life's been nothing but paperwork.
Gustav Mahler

Many carry the Thyrsus but few are inspired
by the Spirit of the God.
Thomas Taylor, the Platonist

Everything's gonna be, all right!
Joe Turner

Some speak of a return to nature — I wonder
where they could have been?
Frederick Sommer

It is a very great mistake to suppose, as a few
English cooks still do, that spaghetti and
macaroni should be soaked in water before
cooking.
Elizabeth David

I thought men like that shot themselves.
King George V

Once, in the army, I was asked if I was really the composer A. S. 'Somebody had to be,' I said, 'and nobody else wanted to, so I took it on, myself.'
Arnold Schoenberg

Critics make *pipi* on music and think they help it grow.
André Gédalge

Success is having to worry about every damn thing in the world, except money.
Johnny Cash

Suffice it to say that increasingly we will encounter one another as enemies, that as individuals we stand more vulnerable to the abrasions we effect on each other. Some of us will flee, to further suburbs and hoped-for havens.
Andrew Hacker

We can be of little service to our fellows until we become disillusioned without being embittered.

F. Fraser Darling

People say you shouldn't be *bitter* when others offer you oaths as perfidious as Cressid's; I think a pint or two of bile is just as essential as voiding, eating, walking, sitting, going to the pissing conduit of old times, or writing.

Edward Dahlberg

Besides — I have seen the door into the back of that hill called Cat Bells — and besides I am very well acquainted with dear Mrs. Tiggy-Winkle.

Beatrix Potter

I think I am beginning to understand something of it.

Auguste Renoir (last words)

III

Alas for the South! Her books have grown
  fewer—
She was never much given to literature.
  The Reverend J. Gordon Cougler

It is one of the few consolations of this planet
that houses cannot move.
  Robert Kelly

Our first questions about the value of a
book, of a human being, or a musical
composition are: Can they walk? Even more,
can they dance?
  Friedrich Nietzsche, from The Gay Science

Come along, he will, some suppertime, for
us, each in turn — and how many even will so
much as look from their play to wave us
good-bye?
  Walter De La Mare

The grass is always greener in other people's
slaughterhouses.
  P. V. Taylor

It's a dangerous business, Frodo, going out of your door.

Bilbo Baggins

A great many people are now what they call modern.

Kate Greenaway (to Ruskin, 1896)

Without the friendship of the Happy Dead, how should we bear our life?

Wall Plaque (Stillingfleet Church, North Yorkshire)

The things we took for granted do not take us so.

Russell Edson

The peculiar grace of a Shaker chair is due to the fact that it was made by someone capable of believing that an angel might come and sit on it.

Thomas Merton

The best thing to do with the better things in life is to give them up.

Dorothy Day

Du Beurre! Donnez-moi du beurre! Toujours du beurre!

Fernand Point

Beauty? Beauty my eye!

Jean Dubuffet

What got you here will get you out of here.

Joe Garagiola

I am still at the heart the dreamy child who used to be found in the reeds by Severn side with a sheet of paper trying to fix the sounds and longing for something very great. I am still looking for this . . . but as a child and as a young man and as a mature man, no single person was ever kind to me.

Sir Edward Elgar

Not only is England an island but so is every
Englishman.

Novalis

Champagne for my sham friends; real pain
for my real friends.

Francis Bacon

Che so io? as the fly said — he was an Italian
fly — when the Hippopotamus asked him
what the moon was made of.

Edward Lear

What, pray, do you do? You walk, my fine
slug, because you are too indolent to english
your feelings . . . Do not think you are a
sphinx because you are a mute.

Edward Dahlberg

Do you think a man who knows his own
value grants anyone the right to criticize even
his most trivial qualities?

Arnold Schoenberg

Never trust a man with a small cock.
Jean Cocteau

The beautiful may be small.
Kant

Laisser l'initiative aux mots!
Mallarmé

A book can be an escape from the house.
Dore Ashton

Beautiful, and smart too.
Ezra Pound (last public words)

Newspapermen ask dumb questions. They look up at the sun and ask you if the sun is shining.
Charles 'Sonny' Liston

Pound thinks he is an anti-Communist. I think I am a Communist. But we both might be mistaken.
Hugh MacDiarmid

Everybody is trying to convince people that kids are interested in ecology, that kids are interested in politics. That's bullshit. Kids are interested in the same things that have always excited them: sex and violence.

Alice Cooper

It's nothing that a guy should take all of his emotions, his prayers and meditations into a night club, and torture the people with their torments by playing everything they feel. It would be better sometimes to play some things they imagine to be true, outside their own personal lives.

Charles Mingus

No occupation is so delightful to me as the culture of the earth, and no culture comparable to that of the garden.

Thomas Jefferson

We do not feel, as Humphrey Repton, the landscape gardener, felt in his epitaph, that our dust is going to turn into roses. Dust we believe simply to be dust.

Geoffrey Grigson

He may be dead; or, he may be teaching English.

Cormac McCarthy

Life to me is not an order into which all things must be brought, but is all things that are alive.

Wesley Huss

Bring all you got!

Bob Gibson

You need travel no further than your own feelings once you have a principle to live by.

Karl Knaths

If there ain't no place to go, there's no way to take a trip.

'Dandy' Don Meredith

Two snakes form the grape arbor. One is giving Eve the apple. The Bible tells all about that. The other snake didn't have any apple, so Adam got hot about it, grabbed it, and is smashing its head with his heel. That shows the disposition of man. If he doesn't get the apple there is something wrong. And the Bible says, the heel of the seed of the woman shall smash the serpent's head—or, something to that effect.

> *S. P. Dinsmoor (creator of 'The Garden of Eden,' Lucas, Kansas)*

No vice is with us the less ridiculous for being in fashion.

> *The United Society of Believers in Christ's Second Appearing*

Fame tends to be a lot of shits thinking you're no longer a threat.

> *Valerie Raworth*

There is hope for us all — if we only get good pitching.

Willard Midgette

There was no sign of survivors, and the poetry reading went on . . .

Tony Perniciaro

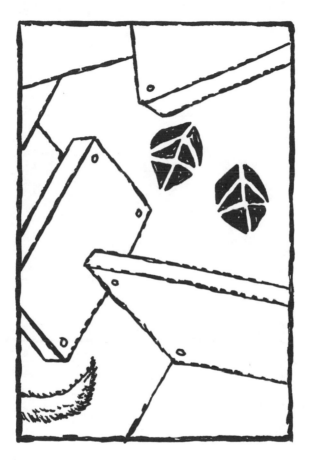

IV

The names of all the 300 I have made myself
acquainted with, because they deserve to be
remembered.

Herodotus

This is an honest book, reader. It warns you
from the outset that in it I have set no goal
but a domestic and private one . . .

Montaigne

There must be five hundred signed copies for
particular friends; six for the general public;
and one for America.

Oscar Wilde

Society is merely everybody else, and you
don't owe everybody anything.

Thomas Berger

There is nothing in nature that is not in us.

Naum Gabo

There are four legs to stand on. The first, be
romantic. The second, be passionate. The
third, be imaginative. And the fourth, never
be rushed.

Charles Olson

Wine tastes like gasoline.

Colonel Harland Sanders

Going to a white-run barbeque is, I think,
like going to a gentile internist: It might turn
out all right, but you haven't made any
attempt to take advantage of the percentages.

Calvin Trillin

One never know, do one?

Thomas Wright Waller

This year I'm smart; in a few seasons I'll
be dumb. But how smart do I have to be
anyway? It's a simple game.

George Lee Anderson

Respectable people do not write music or
make love as a career.

Alexander Porfirevich Borodin

What do I do? I do whatever is to be done
next. I write if I have anything to write.

Virgil Thomson

If you live in the henhouse, you talk to the
hens.

Carlos Toadvine

Trying to sneak a fastball past Henry Aaron
was like trying to sneak the sun past a
rooster.

Curt Simmons

I'd cross an Alp to see a village idiot of
quality.

Norman Douglas

Let's forget it never happened.

Ray Kass

It is a fine thing when a man who thoroughly understands a subject is unwilling to open his mouth.

Yoshida Kenko

Music is yes yes . . . no yes . . . no yes . . .
Charlie Parker

You've got to find some way of saying it without saying it.

Edward Kennedy Ellington

Ask me tomorrow about what it means.
Wesley Unseld

I love you very much but, perhaps, do not tell anyone about it.

Sir James M. Barrie

But everybody knows which comes first when it's a question of cricket or sex—all discerning people recognize that.

Harold Pinter

Use what you got because that's all you get.
Clarence 'Pine Top' Smith

We have no more been able to give full value
to masturbation than we have to
introspection.
James Hilton

I can't go on. I go on.
Samuel Beckett

Nobody knows the way in Concrete Land.
Jeff Nuttall

I'm frankly a bourgeois living in seclusion in
the country, busy with literature and asking
nothing of anyone, not consideration, nor
honour, nor esteem . . . I'd jump into the
water to save a good line of poetry or a good
sentence of prose from anyone. But I don't
believe, on that account, that humanity has
need of me, any more than I have need of it.
Gustave Flaubert

I am but too conscious of the fact that we are born in an age when only the dull are treated seriously, and I live in terror of not being mis-understood.

    Oscar Wilde

Readers — what are they? My books proliferate and are as if they never were.

    Cid Corman

All of us old people have to think that we matter more than others or we would stop storing up on earth such art as moth and rust and Mammon corrupt the shit out of.

    Henry Holmes Smith

City ain't no place for a woman, though a lot of pretty men go there.

    W. C. Fields in The Fatal Glass of Beer

Among the subtle Yaghan concepts Bridges recorded was one which defined 'monotony' as 'an absence of male friends.'

    Bruce Chatwin

When Cartier-Bresson goes to China, he shows that there are people in China, and that they are Chinese.

Susan Sontag

Once a Serbic, always a Serbic.

Anonymous (supplied by David Wilk)

You better make sure you hit my glove exactly where I put it, cause you ain't got diddly-squat tonight.

Thurman Munson

Never kick a fresh turd on a hot day.

Harry S Truman

Take only your imagination seriously.

Thomas Berger

When you photograph a wall, you photograph a wall; when I photograph a wall, I'm photographing something else.

Aaron Siskind

The sun never knew how great it was till it struck the side of a building.

Louis Kahn

I can't answer any questions beginning 'why I'm not as bright as I was, and I've few insights into my motives. I've got some opinions left, probably wrong ones. Ask away.

Adrian Berg

I never expect my friends to be interested in what I do.

R.B. Kitaj

. . . the only hope of our ever getting a really beautiful and vigorous and charming civilization is to allow all the world to fuck and bugger and abuse themselves in public and generally misbehave to their heart's content.

Lytton Strachey

Too much of a good thing is wonderful.

Mae West

There are too many distractions. You should enter a ball park as you would enter a church.

William Francis Lee III

. . . to quote is to name, and naming rather than speaking, the word rather than the sentence, brings truth to light.

Hannah Arendt

. . . it seems as if I've been doing the same things since I was six years old. I'm a few inches taller and I have a graying beard, but otherwise there's not much difference.

Maurice Sendak

On the BBC there has been a spate of obscure XVIIIc English composers, perhaps to show us why they are unknown; and a careful selection of the worst pieces of J. C. Bach set off with nothings by Frederick the Great. As for poetry—and as for readers— the squalor is repulsive.

Basil Bunting

Show yourself more human than critical and
your pleasure will increase.
Domenico Scarletti

You aren't out of it until you're out of it.
Lawrence 'Yogi' Berra

If you're good, you can do it anywhere —
even on the ground with a stick.
Alvin Doyle Moore

As Major Denis Bloodnok exclaimed when
told there were only two sexes: 'It's not
enough, I say.'
R. Albert Hall

His was not a true imagination, you know:
He made it all up.
H. V. G. Dyson (on his friend,
J. R. R. Tolkien)

He who listens hard does not see.
Max Brod

The basic unit for measuring the length,
width and depth is the peter.

> New Orleans Times Picayune *('Start to
> Learn Metric Terms')*

When shit becomes valuable, the poor will be
born without assholes.

> *Brazilian Proverb*

The opera ain't over until the Fat Lady sings!

> *Richard Motta*

V

I am sitting in the smallest room of my house. I have your review before me. In a moment it will be behind me.

Max Reger

The natives were on the whole not very pleasant or very interesting.

Laurence Housman

In fact, you cannot *lead* the Simple Life; it must take you by the hand.

Janet Ashbee

A work of art is a well-made boot.

W. J. Lethaby

Music alone has the power of restoring us to ourselves.

James Gibbons Huneker

The three greatest composers who ever lived are J. S. Bach, Delius, and Duke Ellington.

Percy Alridge Grainger

You can't catch anything in the streets,
except a cold.
Stéphane Grappelli

. . . uh, huh . . . yeah . . .
Miles Davis

Didn't gays used to be a better class of
person?
B. J. Cox

A dozen times in my life I have turned up the
oven.
Judson Crews

He didn't believe in nothing, only what he
wanted to.
*Sheriff Raymond Weatherby (Crane County,
Texas)*

I can't say, over the miles, that I had learned
what I had wanted to know because I hadn't
known what I wanted to know. But I *did*
learn what I didn't know I wanted to know.
William Least Heat Moon

. . . none of Isherwood's moral preoccupations is apt to endear him to a literary establishment that is, variously, academic, Jewish/Christian, middleclass, and heterosexual.

Gore Vidal

There are three kinds of pianists: Jewish pianists, homosexual pianists, and bad pianists.

Vladimir Horowitz

Horrifying things happen nearly every day around here.

Leverett T. Smith (Rocky Mount, North Carolina)

There are two things I like stiff, and one of them's jello.

Dame Nellie Melba

Most things come and go, however good to watch; a few things stay and matter to the end. Rain, for instance . . .

Reynolds Price

It is bad today, and it will be worse
tomorrow; and so on till the worst of all.
Arthur Schopenhauer

Few people have the imagination for reality.
Goethe

People say they have to express their
emotions. I'm sick of that. Photography
doesn't teach you to express your emotions; it
teaches you how to see.
Berenice Abbott

I sincerely believe that the best kind of
criticism is that which is amusing and poetic;
not that cold and algebraic kind which,
under the pretext of explaining everything,
displays neither hate nor love . . .
Charles Baudelaire

No word-person writing on photography has
ever said anything that helped me do better
on Thursday what I'd done less well on
Wednesday.
Ralph Steiner

There must be something in the writings of a man who can attract attention and win applause when corn is thirty cents a bushel and potato bugs have become a burden.

Henry W. Grady (President, The J. Gordon Cougler Fan Club of Atlanta, Georgia)

It doesn't take a big brain to figure out that it's three strikes and you're out.

Red Smith

Don't let the bastards shit on your head. You got a mouth.

Yiddish Adage

To ensure freshness, all foods are cooked from scratch, which is subject to run out.

Dip's County Kitchen (West Rosemary Street, Chapel Hill, North Carolina)

There are lots of things I'm not putting up with anymore, and all attitudes held by artists must be spectacular, undemanding and exemplary.

Simon Cutts

If this sentence were in Chinese, it would say something else.

Douglas R. Hofstadter (cited by)

If my home were on fire and I could take only three records, they would all be *L'Enfant et les Sortilèges*, the most beautiful music ever written.

Ned Rorem

It is very difficult to stop feeling.

Raymond Moore

Be honest with yourself until the end of your life. Then listen to the slow movement of the Schubert *Quintet* and kick the bucket.

Nathan Milstein

When I say boogie-woogie, you shake that thang.

Clarence 'Pine Top' Smith

Look at the typical American family scene: Man walkin' around fartin'. Woman walkin' around scratchin'. Kids goin' around hollerin'. Hey, man, fuck that!

Elvis Presley

Do black-eyed peas — as the tradition says — bring good luck for the coming year? How is it that we believe this, considering our present circumstances? Consider that if we are in this condition after centuries of eating black-eyed peas, what would our condition be if we didn't eat them?

Vertamae Smart-Grosvenor

Because the Jews killed our Lord, they are forever marked with hair on their shoulders — something that no gentile man has on *his* shoulders except for John Travolta and a handful of other Italian-Americans from the Englewood, New Jersey area.

Gore Vidal

The war was like pro football in that mostly niggers and rednecks and Slovenians fought it and the rest of us watched.

Roy Blount, Jr., from Crackers

We were here when you were out and if you would like to know more about a visit Christ make to America soon after his resurrection in Jerusalem, call 497-4092.

Elder Croghan, Elder Davis (Laguna Beach, California)

He snarled at everyone, screaming '*Esel*' at one, '*Scheisshund*' to another, '*Dreck*' to all — a dirty, foul, dark man.

Frau Meinander (landlady to L. von Beethoven)

You know who help me make this coyote? God, that's the one, no one else. And I try the best I can, that's all you can do. If I was any better, I'd have to be a regular artist, a real McCoy.

Felipe Archuleta (Santa Cruz, New Mexico)

Art is always the replacement of indifference by attention.

Guy Davenport

The first poetry is always written by sailors and farmers who sing with the wind in their teeth. The second poetry is written by scholars and students, wine drinkers who have learned to know a good thing. The third poetry is sometimes never written; but when it is, it is written by those who have brought nature and art into one thing.

Walter Anderson

Goodness me, when Giotto was painting his murals of the Life of Christ at Padua, he wasn't thinking of me! And it certainly means something to me. I think that thinking too much about communicating and making the work mean something to others is a sure way of having it mean nothing at all to anybody.

Norman Adams

I hated music and I still do. What I love is sound.

Bruce Hampton (aka Hampton B. Coles, Ret.)

Sonny boy, it's all real — so watch out!

The Town Drunk of Tarboro, North Carolina

VI

An 'alcoholic' is a man you don't like, who
drinks as much as you do.
Dylan Thomas

There are people who take the heart out of
you, and there are people who put it back.
Elizabeth David

The struggle was and still might be, to
preserve some of the values that make life
worth living. And they are still mousing
around for a significance in the chaos.
Ezra Pound

Never put pen to paper!
Lady Ida Sitwell

The great thing is to go empty to the grave.
*Reno Odlin, quoting Hollis Frampton (?),
Yeats (?) . . .*

I think the trouble with this country is that
there is a lot of the Belgrano Spirit — hurray
for me, fuck you.
Tony Marchant

. . . Fear those prepared to die for the truth,
for as a rule they will make others die with
them . . . Perhaps the mission of those who
love mankind is to make people laugh at the
truth, *to make truth laugh*, because the only
truth lies in learning to free ourselves from
this insane passion for the truth.

> *William of Baskerville, in* The Name of
> the Rose *by Umberto Eco*

' . . . THE PRICE OF PRIDE IS HIGH,
AND PAID BY THE YOUNG . . .'

> *On the German War Memorial, El Alamein,
> Egypt*

In Suburbia they thump you for anything
. . . People still think heteros make love and
gays have sex. I want to tell them that's
wrong.

> *Boy George (Alan O'Dowd)*

The purpose of sexual intercourse is to get it
over with as long as possible.

> *Steven Max Singer*

Like Blake, John Betjeman feared both pretension and learning (as opposed to knowledge), seeing them both as destructive of feeling, as substitutes for the eye, the ear and the heart.

Myfanwy Piper

Get along, says our DNA, talk to each other, figure out the world, be useful, and above all keep an eye out for affection.

Lewis Thomas, M.D.

It doesn't matter what anybody tells you. Now shut up and listen!

Francis Phelan, in Ironweed *by William Kennedy*

If you have to eat crow, eat it while it's hot.

Alben Barkley, Vice President of the United States

Tome mucho café, fume un buen cigarro, y no se ocupe. (Drink a lotta coffee, smoke a good cigar, and don't fret yourself.)

The World's Oldest Peruvian, circa aet. 165

I trust you know the 'Three Nevers for Proper Gentlemen'?
NEVER SHOOT SOUTH OF THE THAMES . . .
NEVER FOLLOW WHISKY WITH PORT . . .
NEVER HAVE YOUR WIFE IN THE MORNING —
THE DAY MAY HAVE SOMETHING BETTER TO
OFFER . . .

P. V. Taylor

I don't know where jazz is going. Maybe it's going to hell. You can't make anything go anywhere. It just happens.

Thelonious Sphere Monk

YOU'LL GET IT WHEN YOU GET IT
Embroidered Jockstrap (Kent, Ohio)

Always carry a corkscrew and the wine shall provide itself.

Basil Bunting

REMEMBER TO DIE!
The Gospel, According to the Reverend Eldren M. Bailey

ACT SINCERE, EVEN IF YOU DON'T MEAN IT
Shopping Mall Sign (Acworth, Georgia)

I must rejoice beyond bounds of time . . .
though the world may shudder at my joy, and
in its coarseness know not what I mean.

   Jan van Ruysbroeck

Read all the great poems, plays and novels
that you can, for Dante will lead you into the
dramatic economy of Giotto, Racine will help
you feel the balanced organization of
Poussin, Flaubert will show you how the
Impressionists looked at life. *The more you
know, the more you see.* Read general history,
the history of science, of economics, of ideas,
for these, like the history of art, are all peek
holes into the central mystery of man. Any
one approach, if pursued without reference
to others, dwindles into something like 19th
century theology—a complex dissertation
about nothing in particular.

   A. Hyatt Mayor

People of that class did not like to touch doorknobs.

> *The Doorman (for 62 years) at*
> *Henri Bendel's*

Every man is his own equal!

> *Rick Flair (Mid-Atlantic Professional*
> *Wrestling Champion)*

When I went to New York in the airplane, I saw a picture in the clouds and I got my pencil right out. I drew something with a long tail and horns.

> *Nellie Mae Rowe*

When things get too unpleasant, I burn the day's newspaper, pull down the curtains, get out the jugs, and put in a civilized evening.

> *H. L. Mencken*

What the good Christian people of this country need is TIGHT PUSSY, LOOSE SHOES, AND A WARM PLACE TO SHIT. Don't knock it, good buddy!

> *The Reverend A. Jarry Foulwool*

His worm dieth not, and his fire is
unquenched!

Diabolic Variations on a Theme by Isaiah

In art the same elevator goes either to the
basement or the penthouse.

Piet Mondrian

The old new music began before our time, in
the incunabula of Satie, Debussy, Schoenberg,
and Stravinsky—you may throw in (out)
Bartok (hammer hammer hammer) and
Hindemith (no sex?) . . . All art, even
Hindemith, even Satie, even Poulenc, is sad,
so sad and lost.

James Sellars

Whenever I go to a restaurant I don't know,
I always ask to meet the chef before I eat.
For I know that if he is thin, I won't eat well.
And if he is thin *and* sad, there is nothing for
it but to run. (But, before misjudging a thin
man, one should make an enquiry or two—
he may be a formerly fat man.)

Fernand Point

We should live as if we were never going to
die, for it is the deaths of our friends that
hurt us, not our own.

Gerald Brenan

Insanity did not just *run* in the Queensberrys;
it galloped apace — the third Marquess
even turned his hand to cannibalism
(he cooked a member of the kitchen staff
and was discovered tucking in).

Bernard Levin

I struggled for 47 years, I distinguished
myself in every way I possibly could. I never
had a compliment nor a 'Thank you', nor a
single farthing. I translated a doubtful book
in my old age, and I immediately made
16,000 guineas. Now that I know the tastes
of England, we never be without money . . .
The deadly shade of respectability, the trail
of the slow-worm, is over them all.

Sir Richard Burton

All cucumbers should be sandwiched: no other use is imaginable.

P. V. Taylor

Dear boy, it isn't that your manners are bad—it's simply that you have no manners at all.

Margot Asquith

If I lived there, I'd move.

The Divine Sarah Vaughan
(On the liberality of the City of Boston)

Insects are so mechanical we don't consider they might include a few eccentrics.

Colin Simms

Religion is what a man does with his solitude.

Alfred North Whitehead

A thing just comes — or it doesn't — usually doesn't.

Ralph Vaughan Williams

The opening of the piece (Shostakovich, *Symphony No. 5*) spoke immediately of music smarting under the lashes of its idea. They dug their nails into its taut rhythmic pacing, and undergirded the Largo's occasional longueurs with cello playing of unusually distinctive character and tenacity. Where double entendre masquerades as single entendre in this work, extremity becomes, as it should, not only the means but the mode, and did so utterly convincingly.

Hilary Finch, The London Times

Some people are so ignorant they wouldn't know how to pour piss out of a boot — even if the instructions were printed on the heel.

President Lyndon Baines Johnson

Lives devoted to Beauty seldom end well.

Sir Kenneth Clark (on Shannon & Ricketts)

A timid temperament helps; a little goes a long way; a couple of air raids do wonders for you.

Christopher Isherwood

Try to enjoy as much as you can. Try to enjoy as much as you can.

J. B. Priestley

There are two kinds of writers, those who are and those who aren't. With the first, content and form belong together like soul and body; with the second, they match each other like body and clothes.

Karl Kraus

Even in these decadent days almost every schoolboy knows that the French speak French instead of English.

John P. Harris

Art never seems to make me peaceful or pure.

Willem de Kooning

If you keep straight you will have no friends but catgut and blossom in season.

Basil Bunting, from Chomei at Toyama

I can't help hearing what I hear.
Ray Gosling

I only know what people tell me.
Lew Archer, in The Wycherley Woman *by Ross Macdonald*

We didn't have nothin' goin', but it still went.
Edgar Tolson (1904–1984)

There's no use in the world fretting about things that don't matter. We all get to the hillside eventually.
Dewitt Chatham Hanes

Ah, dear boy, you know what happens when drink is taken.
P. V. Taylor

One does not wish to be paid for writing a love letter.
A. Wainwright

'I've always been a man of God,' he replied, chewing another cookie. 'God's green, and he folds.'

Augustus Krepsin, in Mystery Walk *by Robert McCammon*

Rejoice in the things that are present; all else is beyond thee.

Montaigne

Build, therefore, your own world.

Ralph Waldo Emerson

We have, I think, come quite a long way in quite a short time . . . It is *much* worse to blow people up with bombs than to smash their windows, spit upon their children, daub their houses with obscenities and put them, night and day, in fear. But great though the difference is, it is still the difference between a large horse and a small horse, not a horse and a cow. Large or small, the horses have got loose, and they are galloping about Britain. They had better be corralled soon.

Bernard Levin

Ah, the working classes of England . . .
Lovely in bed; not too good standing up.

P. V. Taylor

What dull barbarians are not proud of their
dullness and barbarism?

Thackeray

His Majesty does not know what the Band
has just played, but it is never to be played
again!

King George V

VII

I wouldn't vote for a Republican even if
Jesus Christ claimed to be one.

Judge Jim Shipman, Henderson County,
North Carolina

It *is* glory, to have been tested, to have had
our little quality and cast our little spell. The
thing is to have made somebody care.

Henry James

There are places in the heart which might
have been gardens, or favorite quarters,
around which we have built high walls,
whose doors have been shut too long.

Guy Davenport, from Apples & Pears

I wonder what they'll do when they get to
Heaven, where there's music no one heard
of? Are they going to walk off? I don't think
they'll get in.

Thomas Jefferson Jarrell, fiddler, Round
Mountain, Toenail Gap, North Carolina

Find out who they are. And then kick ass!
Elmore Leonard, from 52 Pick-Up

Life is a shit sandwich. But, man, if you've
got enough bread, you don't taste the shit.
> *Jonathan Winters*

. . . Homosexuals do not normally follow
men who offer dicks that appear to be no
bigger than a ziti macaroni.
> *The Reverend Boyd McDonald*

A woman without a man is like a fish without
a bicycle.
> *Florynce Kennedy*

It's just like it always is.
> *Chandler Gordon*

I was now breathing the politist atmosphere
in America. These people never moved but in
a carriage, lolled on sophas instead of sitting
on chairs, and were always attended by their
Negroes to fan them with a peacock's feather.
> *John Davis, (Ashley River plantations, South
> Carolina, 1799)*

Coons are either funny — or dangerous.
Harold Ross, Founding Editor of the New Yorker

My wife's got some injun in her, she likes to boil taters, sit in a tent, and keep to herself.
The Reverend Howard Finster

A man who thinks he is building a home is really building a tavern for his friends.
Norman Douglas

If you fuck a bull, you get bullshit on your prick.
Paul Goodman

A paranoid is a man who knows a little of what's going on.
William Burroughs

It is always wise to tip well on the way up in case you meet the same dreary, greedy cunts on the way down.
P. V. Taylor

It infuriates me to be wrong when I know
I'm right.
Molière

The world is forwarded by having its
attentions fixed on the best things.
Matthew Arnold

Peace isn't even as good a sales item as
poetry.
W. H. Ferry

New York City isn't easy. Bring a fur!
Vogue, October, 1985

Whatever the masses are, I got no plans to be
one of them.
Dona Brown

In those days I wished to seem more
interesting than I knew myself to be . . .
Now, I turn many fewer heads than I
used to.
David Sherwood

I guess when you turn off the main road, you have to be prepared to see some funny houses.

Stephen King, from Rage

I much prefer being a man. Women have to spend so much time pulling themselves together, and their shoes kill your feet. I know.

Mister Lynne Carter

If I'd've hit that many singles, I'd've wore a dress!

Mickey Mantle, 1985, reflecting on Pete Rose's surpassing Ty Cobb's hitting record

I should've been a preacher. I like pussy and fried chicken as well as anybody.

Carlos Toadvine (aka Little Enis)

There is nothing inherently un-American about taste.

Orcenith Lyle Bongé

. . . it is at table that everything happens.
Pierre du Bussac

Too much passivity these days, people are
always waiting for a leader . . . Never wait,
just vote for the least imbecile of the lot and
continue griping and create whatever
microcosm of perfection you can in your own
life . . .
Andre Monestier

If we had a keen vision and feeling of all
ordinary human life, it would be like hearing
the grass grow and the squirrel's heart beat,
and we should die of that roar which lies on
the other side of silence.
George Eliot

As long as we tolerate the division of
Mankind into power & profit organizations
and nations all continuously at one another's
throats, we must each remind ourselves that
though it is beautiful, each day is miserable.
And act accordingly.
John Cage

War and cruelty apart, it is no longer a laughing matter to be a member of the human race.

Jeffrey Bernard

. . . the fact that many people prefer bad art to good art is not a matter for criminal prosecution but an ingredient in the human comedy, one by which other people will always know how to profit.

John Russell

I'LL HAE NAE HAUFWAY HOOSE, BUT AYE BE
    WHAUR
EXTREMES MEET— IT'S THE ONLY WAY I KEN
TO DODGE THE CURSED CONCEIT O' BEIN'
    RICHT
THAT DAMNS THE VAST MAJORITY O' MEN
    Hugh MacDiarmid, epitaph, Langholm,
    Dumfriesshire, Scotland

Poetry always was, and always should be, pre-eminently that: significant sound.

D.G. Bridson

To me, apples are fruit — to Cézanne they
were mountains!

> *David Smith*

I certainly *do* hate the act of painting: &
although day after day, I go steadily on, it is
like grinding my nose off.

> *Edward Lear*

She'd make you eat a mile of her shit, just to
get a whiff of her asshole.

> *John Gilbert, on The Divine Garbo*

There are no words to express the abyss
between isolation and having one ally. It may
be conceded to the mathematicians that four
is twice two. But two is not twice one; two is
two thousand times one . . .

> *G.K. Chesterton*

I've lost friends because I don't see them:
they've changed, they're not there anymore.

> *Orson Welles*

God be with you, my dears. You keep the old bugger. I shan't be needing him!

Norman Douglas, last words

... the best reason for a young writer to meet an older writer is the possibility that he might learn a few manners. Practically everything of consequence is in the work.

Russell Banks

The way to write is well, and how is your own business.

A. J. Liebling

... Owing to tempestuous weather, it may be impossible to heave the lead or observe the heavenly bodies.

Jonathan Williams, Philadelphia, 1799

There is perhaps only one place where it is socially acceptable for a human being to give in to all his primal urges while driving an automobile: Boston, Massachusetts.

The Boston Driver's Handbook: Wild In The Streets

I'm not surprised that you can round up a
lynch mob. We were always able to do that in
this country.

*Benjamin Ward, Police Commissioner of
New York City*

My God! What an awful place!
*Robert Falcon Scott, on first seeing the
South Pole, April, 1912*

. . . by then I had known for many years that
in a democracy it is frequently necessary to
enter the polling booth holding one's nose.

Bernard Levin

Nothing short of being caught in bed with a
dead girl or a live boy can hurt my political
career in this state.

Edwin C. Edwards, Governor of Louisiana

It's always night or we wouldn't need light.
Theolonious Sphere Monk

Three things in human life are important.
The first is to be kind. The second is to be
kind. And the third is to be kind.

Henry James

The most fearful and dangerous thing in the
world is not a lion on the loose or an atom
bomb in its silo, but a *closed* mind.

Michael Seide

There are as many fools in the world as there
are people.

Sigmund Freud

. . . I'd go to the city quite often to try to
learn new ideas, but I never learned a thing.

Enos 'Country' Slaughter

There's more to life than sunlight on water,
tits, a pâpier-maché death's head, and fanny
on horseback, shot through a lens full of
vaseline.

Stuart Mills

You know . . . I love Nature. I just don't
want to get any on me!

> *Roxanne Martin (urban fox visiting the Blue
> Grass)*

MUSIC COLUMNIST: Have you ever heard any
Stockhausen?

SIR THOMAS BEECHAM: No, not at all. But, I
believe I have stepped in some.

Ramps are synonymous with spring. Ramps
go with changing the oil or your underwear.

> *Jim Comstock, Editor,* The West Virginia
> Hillbilly

In summer, a gentleman is never far from a
bottle of chilled beaujolais.

> *Mado Point, Restaurant de la Pyramide,
> Vienne, France*

What was was was! What is is is!

> *Sparky Anderson, 1986*

He was an egotist, a solitary, in his pleasures; he used to contend that no garden on earth, however spacious, was large enough for more than one man.

Norman Douglas, from South Wind

VIII

IF YOU DON'T LIKE MY DRIVING
DIAL 1-800-EAT-SHIT

> *State-of-the-art bumper sticker, Jackson, Mississippi*

At the *Hungry Horse* the cooking is a Spanish or Italian or Malaysian idea of English home-cooking—which is at least preferable to the English idea of English home-cooking.

> *Jonathan Meades*, The London Times

The artist has no right to waste the time of his listener.

> *Erik Alfred Leslie Satie*

In the final analysis, however, opera is a poor substitute for baseball.

> The Los Angeles Herald, *October 12, 1986*

An artist should be fit for the best society and keep out of it.

> *John Ruskin*

I hope that no matter what happens to you, I hope you can't smell it, taste it, or fuck it.

> *Police Chief Mario Balzic, in* The Man Who Liked Slow Tomatoes, *by K. C. Constantine*

Beauty never lasts in this world. God and man and large dogs see to that.

> *Kinky Friedman, from* Greenwich Killing Time

ERNIE, THE BOYFRIEND: Soph, the trouble with you is you've got no tits and a tight box.

SOPHIE TUCKER, LAST OF THE RED-HOT MAMAS: Ernie, get off my back!

Warhol is significant because he showed us our culture was a total zero — that a rectum could be portrayed as a flower. They'd smell it and not know the difference between a rectum and a flower.

> *James Purdy*

There's more money in being commercial.

> *Wladziu Valentino Liberace*

Now God refused to come down to earth in the form of potato flour: that was an undeniable, indisputable fact.

J.K. Huysmans

Although our information is incorrect, we do not vouch for it.

Erik Alfred Leslie Satie

It was one of those perfect English autumnal days which occur more frequently in memory than in life.

P.D. James, from A Taste for Death

We English are good at forgiving our enemies; it releases us from the obligation of liking our friends.

P.D. James, from Shroud for a Nightingale

You know what a friend is? Someone who knows all about you and likes you anyway.

Duane Charles Parcells

The public seems to want me to dance — and so I dance.

Raymond Wallace Bolger

Nothing is more evident than that Nature hates Mind. Thinking is the most unhealthy thing in the world, and people die of it just as they die of any other disease. Fortunately, in England at any rate, thought is not catching.

Oscar Wilde

LOVE, and do what you will.

St. Augustine

People know what they do; they frequently know why they do what they do; but what they don't know is what what they do does.

Michel Foucault

Those who love something passionately are more likely to be right than those who don't.

Yehudi Menuhin

You have eyes outside and eyes inside. Your heart is full of eyes. To communicate, you put the two together. Amen!

Dilmus Hall

Tutti Frutti, good booty/If it don't fit, don't force it/You can grease it, make it easy . . . AWOP-BOP-A-LOO-MOP ALOP-BAM-BOOM!

Richard Wayne Penniman, 1955

Let him among us who has neither ass nor pain come forward!

Iron City Steve, in Always a Body to Trade, *by K. C. Constantine*

And with the guts of the last priest, let us strangle the last king.

Denis Diderot

I believe in Original Sin. I find people profoundly bad and irresistibly funny.

Joe Orton

Mr. Wordsworth wasn't a man as was thowte
a deal o' for his potry when he was
hereabout. It hed no laugh in it . . . It was
kept oer long in his heead mappen . . . It was
aw reet eneuf but queer stuff, varra . . .

> *H. D. Rawnsley (considerations of the Poet
> Laureate by yeomen and peasants in the
> Dales, from Literary Associations of the
> English Lakes)*

Since God has given me a cheerful heart, He
will forgive me for serving Him cheerfully.

> *Franz Joseph Haydn*

Music cannot be harmless. It is one of the
most secret means we have of expressing our
situation here on this earth.

> *Kurt Schwertsik*

The one way of tolerating existence is to lose
oneself in literature as in a perpetual orgy
. . . (The minute I no longer have a book on
hand or am not dreaming of writing one, I
could *howl* with boredom.)

> *Gustave Flaubert*

If you can kill a snake with it, it ain't art.
Orcenith Lyle Bongé

The only thing one can be proud of is of
having worked in such a way that an official
reward for your labor cannot be envisaged by
anyone.
Jean Cocteau

Every land you walked was you, and you
were never alone.
Ibn-al-Arabi

At the end of his life the hero of *An Obscure
Man* isn't quite sure if he is a man or a
woman, an animal or a plant. I feel this way.
I don't feel that the difference between men
and women is at all important.
Marguerite Yourcenar

To look is to forget the name of the things
you are seeing.
Paul Valéry

Good verses alwayes doe Require
A vacant mind, & sweet Retire.

> *Thomas Traherne, from* Groves, *a newly
> published essay*

More and more I feel bent against the
modern English habit of using poetry as a
channel for thinking aloud, instead of making
anything.

> *Matthew Arnold*

I sigh for the pestilential breath of an African
serpent to destroy every Englishman who
comes in my way.

> *William Beckford*

The whole dream of democracy is to raise the
proletarian to the level of stupidity attained
by the bourgeois.

> *Gustave Flaubert*

The English are not a very spiritual people,
so they invented cricket to give them some
idea of eternity.

> *George Bernard Shaw*

Western Civilization went out to take a shit
and the pigs ate it!
  Walter P. Ater

I told Jimmy Carter that Reagan's got just
what this country wants: a good head o' hair
and a mean line o' talk!

ST. EOM OF THE LAND OF PASQUAN

'To my mind there's no finer sight than kale
moving at speed,' opined Millward.
  Glen Baxter

You're gonna lose some ballgames and
you're gonna win some ballgames and that's
about it.
  Sparky Anderson

For whatever Dear Readers there are now,
or are to come, Edward Dahlberg wrote 18
books and one masterpiece that will endure;
at the end of his long life he had less than six
people he would have called friend.
  William O'Rourke

What can be shown cannot be said.
Ludwig Wittgenstein

When I sell a man a good book, I am the happy transmitter of a precious thing and I feel I have justly earned my profit.
Jacob Zeitlin

Morty Feldman once referred to the Jewish doctor Semmelweiss, who was apparently stoned in the street because he asked his colleagues to wash their hands before delivering babies, and asked to be identified with him. Composers, he thought, should wash out their ears before composing.
Peter Dickinson

At his best Elvis Presley didn't do a lot: he didn't drink, he didn't smoke, and he didn't swear. According to Natalie Wood, who refrained from saying what else he didn't do, dating him was like being back in High School.
Stephen Games, The Independent, *London*

About Schoenberg's 12-tone system, John Coltrane said: 'Damn the rules. It's the feeling that counts. You play all 12 notes anyway.' He had not worn underwear since he was 18.

Mike Zwerin

Claude Debussy played the piano with the lid down.

Robert Bresson

When jazz becomes confounded with art, passion flies out and pretension flies in. I believe that what people in time come to see as the important art of a period always was created out of a wish to act directly and immediately on the real feelings of people — to persuade, influence, entertain, disturb, amuse, or excite at least some people. Duke Ellington's best work was created to do just that.

James Lincoln Collier

Do not imagine that Art is something which is designed to give gentle uplift and self-confidence. Art is not a brassière. At least, not in the English sense. But do not forget that brassière is the French for *life jacket.*

Julian Barnes, from Flaubert's Parrot

The Art of Discourse, whether in verse or prose, lies only in words, not in ideas . . . ideas are common to all, and are at the disposal of every understanding, to employ as it will, needing no art.

Ibn Khaldun

Mr. William Barnes, in his poems, is nothing but a poet. He does not there protest against anything in religion, politics, or the arrangements of society; nor has he the advantage of being able to demand the admiration of the sympathizing public on the score that he is a chimney sweep, or a rat catcher, and has never learned to read.

Coventry Patmore

Across the wires the electric message came,
'HE IS NO BETTER. HE IS MUCH THE SAME.'

> *Alfred Austin, Poet Laureate (on the illness of the Prince of Wales)*

The cold douche of T. S. Eliot had not washed over the warm and precious velvet of those lawns, still less the outlandish flotsam of Ezra Pound.

> *Laurence Whistler, from* The Laughter and the Urn

I tend to prefer the more unclad tribes of the North American Indian.

> *Sir William Ackroyd*

Even the most generous and benign souls might find it hard to enthuse about pottery.

> *Robin Dutt,* The Independent, *London*

In the depths of my heart I can't help being convinced that my dear fellowmen, with a few exceptions, are worthless.

> *Sigmund Freud*

Books are where things are explained to you;
life is where things aren't. I'm not surprised
some people prefer books. Books make sense
of life. The only problem is that the lives they
make sense of are other people's lives, never
your own.

Julian Barnes, from Flaubert's Parrot

There was a man afloat in days. Believing
wisdom comes with time. He lived through
people, cars, and dogs in a house of tarpaper
stone.

Jack Earl

I am at home everywhere and nowhere.
Marguerite Yourcenar

SHIT HAPPENS!
*Herakleitan bumper sticker, New Orleans,
Louisiana*

DOO-DOO HAPPENS
*Simpering, mealy-mouthed bumper sticker,
Atlanta, Georgia*

108

EXCREMENT OCCURS POSSIBLY
Imaginary bumper sticker, London, England

If your cock's as big as your mouth, honey,
I'll see you after the show.
Mae West (to a heckler)

Listen, hot stuff, I'm more woman than you'll
ever get and more man than you'll ever be!
Divine

To get a better piece of chicken, you'd have
to be a rooster.
Mickey Mantle's Country Cookin' Inc.

The only thing God *didn't* do to Job was give
him a computer.
I. F. Stone

I love people to a certain extent. But
sometimes I want to get off in the garden to
talk with God. I have the blooms, and when
the blooms are gone, I love to watch the
green. God dressed the world in green.
Minnie Evans

I LOVE A GARDEN THAT IS A GOD
Sign in the garden of Mary Tillman Smith,
Hazelhurst, Mississippi

Nobody is coming after us.
Nipper Kapirigi, last keeper of the Stories of
the Dreamtime for the Gagudju aborigines,
Kakadu Park, Australia

. . . Language is a deluge from one small
corner of the heart . . . The shuttle has
worked in my heart as it worked in the hearts
of those who came before me . . . The stream
we muddy soon runs itself clean again . . . It
comes from rain like clouds . . .
Lu Chi, from Wen Fu *(Sam Hamill's*
translation)

LETTERS is designed as a book of
primaries, a book of companions, a book
of praises. I have stored here, as best I
know how, the song of what I live by. For
I adhere to form as the bee obeys the
geometry of his hive.
Robert Duncan

110

There are no wrong notes!
Thelonious Sphere Monk

Mozart died too late rather than too soon.
Glenn Gould

A system of knowledge is always also a
system of ignorance.
Terry Tafoya

As for me, all I know is nothing.
Socrates

IX

This sparkling poetry is very dry, light, fruity and well-balanced. Excellent for any occasion, anywhere.

Variations on Freixenet's 'Cordon Negro Brut' label

I do not think one can ever really feel anything for people who have no faith in one, while conversely I believe that one could die with the greatest pleasure for those who do have it . . .

Isak Dinesen, from a letter to her mother

And then I think that unless one is oneself one cannot do anything much for others. With the best will in the world and even with a great deal of effort, one will always to a certain extent give them stones instead of bread — and both sides know it.

Isak Dinesen, from a letter to her mother

The only thing that makes me feel *Jewish* is anti-semitism.

Pierre Mendes France

For what do we live, but to make sport for
our neighbours, and laugh at them in our
turn.

    Jane Austen

A work in which there are theories is like an
object which still has the ticket that shows its
price.

    Marcel Proust

I am not one who believes that a man has to
show his religious party card before one can
speak to him . . . God asks of us, first of all,
sincerity and truth. Conformity is not the
first requisite, or the second, or the tenth. I
do not know where it may stand on the list,
or whether it is on the list at all, since God
has not shown me His list. But since He has
made us for the truth, it stands to reason that
we have to be true in order to know the
truth.

    Thomas Merton (letter to Steve Eisner)

I know everything. One has to, to write decently.

Henry James

Food is never just something to eat.

Margaret Visser, from Much Depends On Dinner

. . . not even the potato chip route man from Nashville would be coming. Friday-night-date-night, and Bea thought of the snake in the rockpile.

Jere Cunningham, from The Abyss

. . . the school we were at together wasn't a particularly good one. Long on sodomy and things but a bit short on the straight bat, honour and other expensive extras, although they talked a lot about them in Chapel. Cold baths a-plenty, of course, but you, who have never taken one, may be surprised to learn that your actual cold bath is your great begetter of your animal passions.

The Honorable Charlie Mortdecai, in Don't Point That Thing At Me, *by Kyril Bonfiglioli*

In our darkness, there is not a place for
beauty. Every place is for beauty.

    René Char

It takes guts to be a fairy in the perpetual
war zone. Robert Duncan showed us a thing
or two.

    Michael Rumaker

The price for anything is what someone will
pay for it.

    Jean-Michel Cazes (Chateau Lynch-Bages)

Baseball saves me every time — not the news
of it, perhaps, so much as its elegant and
arduous complexity, its layered substrata of
nuance and lesson and accumulated
experience . . .

    Roger Angell

The heart is deceitful above all things, &
desperately wicked: who can know it?

    Jeremiah

I declare myself a Morave, with this
Moravian, just as I tried to persuade the
priest at Our Lady of the Snows that I was,
in essential things, a Catholic; it is not my
fault if they put me out, I continue to knock
at the door, I will be in; there is no sect in
the world I do not count mine.

> *Robert Louis Stevenson, from* Travels With
> a Donkey

You know what they say: as soon as your
face clears up, your mind goes.

> *Ellen Patterson (aka Ford Betty Ford)*

I don't think there are any sins; I think there
are things you don't admit, look into, or
confront, so confrontation is my response.

> *Robert Duncan*

Socrates told his students to know
themselves. He couldn't guarantee that they
had the equipment.

> *Antisthenes*

Odilon Redon may have been a hermit, but
he knew the train schedules.

> *Edgar Degas*

I would like to hear Elliott Carter's *Fourth
String Quartet*, if only to discover what a
cranky prostate does to one's polyphony.

> *James Sellars*

Some people can make biscuits better than
others.

> *Clinton Dockery, The Lantern, Dobson,
> North Carolina*

I'm liable to dream anything. That gives you
in your head what to do. Then you get up
and try. If you can't hold it in your head, you
can't do it in your hand.

> *James 'Son' Thomas*

I may be ignorant, but I'm not stupid!

> *Loretta Lynn*

O, well, you win some, you lose some, but
you gotta get dressed for 'em all.

    Susan Kenney, from Graves in Academe

My retirement from teaching was a most
blessed event. Five years, and I still thrive on
the absence of students. For me most of them
were like the blight was to Irish potatoes 134
years ago.

    Henry Holmes Smith

The shorter and the plainer the better.

    Beatrix Potter

Well, you know, I was at one time of my life
a compositor, and when a compositor gets to
the end of his stick, he stops short and goes
ahead on the next line. I aim at making my
verse all neat and pretty on the pages, like
the epitaph on a square tombstone . . .

    *Walt Whitman (talking prosody with
Oscar Wilde)*

Very few of us can own things without being corrupted by them, gaining thereby a false security! Very few of us can resist being distracted by things. We need to choose the simple and lasting instead of the new and individual . . . This means reducing instead of adding, the reversal of our habitual thinking.

Anni Albers

Longing performs all things.

Mary Renault, from The Persian Boy

The poet's only responsibility is to write fresh lines.

Charles Olson

Man thrives where angels die of ecstasy and pigs die of disgust. The contemporary situation is like a long-standing, fatal disease. It is impossible to recall what life was like without it. We seem always to have had cancer of the heart.

Kenneth Rexroth

Poetry is nobody's business except the poet's, and everybody else can fuck off.

Philip Larkin

If it is hard to believe in God, it is no easier to believe in man.

Margot Asquith

If artists need models to admire, let them follow Rilke's example and try to draw and labor like Cézanne, the old man of Aix, in spite of whatever stones the local children — or the metropolitan pundits — chuck at them. Then, when they are tempted to vanity and are invited to conferences and chat-shows, they will decline the crested bait and get back to work. It is a lonely and unglamorous formula, but there is no other . . . The only real hope is to be able to go on working. 'Travaillons,' Cézanne would say, when visitors wanted to talk aesthetics.

Frederic Raphael

All sickness ain't death, Mister Lyle, and
what won't kill will fatten.

A. G. Hilton

I avoided or repelled undesirable intimacies.
I remember that a middle-aged homosexual
novelist, whom I had met only twice and
whose name I have now forgotten, said to
me, 'May I call you Joe? I said, 'No.' I was
out not to give pleasure but to get it.

J.R. Ackerley, from My Father and
Myself

I thought that once you turned 60 that your
balls shrivelled to the size of cat gonads, that
your pubic hair hung down like spanish
moss, and that you needed a nailfile to find
your weenie. I find no abating whatsoever of
lust. That seems as indestructible as one's
toenails, and will probably continue on in the
grave!

Robert Peters

Finding a business man interested in the arts is like finding chicken shit in the chicken salad.

Alice Neel

I am for an art that is political-erotical-mystical, that does something else other than sit on its ass in a museum . . . I am for an art that grows up not knowing that it is art at all, an art given the chance of having a starting point of zero . . .

Claes Oldenburg, from Store Days

Nec humane laudis amore, nec temporalis premii cupiditate . . . sed in augmentum honoris et gloriae nominis Dei. (Not for the love of human praise, not for the desire of earthly reward . . . but to increase the honor and glory of God.)

Theophilus, Bishop of Antioch

Deliver us from Good and Evil!

Aleister Crowley

I would not claim, as I used to, that poetry can change the weather. But, at least it is something to *do*, as reader or writer, when under the cloud.

Thomas A. Clark

A man should stand in awe of his prejudices, as of aged parents and monitors. They may in the end prove wiser than he.

William Hazlitt

Art has to be forgotten: Beauty must be realized.

Piet Mondrian

A really nasty nation can and should produce a really nasty press, but it is the nation we should detest—and, in my case, enjoy detesting—before the newspapers which mirror it.

Auberon Waugh

England is a Jew-owned deer park, with tea rooms.

Ezra Pound (wrong again and right again)

We went to a grand party in the Agnellis'
vast, vast palace in Turin . . . Danny was
sitting next to the Queen of Denmark, and
she asked him if he had ever been to Europe
before. 'No,' he said, 'except for that time in
Korea.' I was sitting across the table and
heard every word, and I laughed until the
tears came to my eyes. Marella liked him,
but didn't know how dumb he was. To
Europeans like that all Americans are the
same. We're all niggers. They don't see any
difference because they think we're totally
unimportant. You can pass anyone off on
them.

> *Truman Capote (né Truman Streckfus
> Persons)*

GRASP TIME AND LEARN TO KNOW THE
WORLD.

> *Dutch proverb (engraved on an oboe by
> Hendrik Richters)*

I forgive everyone and I ask for everyone's
forgiveness. OK? Don't gossip too much.

> *Cesare Pavese (suicide note, August 1950)*

Painting is like hand-stuffing a mattress.
   Franz Kline

I would like to live in Manchester, England.
The transition between Manchester and
death would be unnoticeable.
   Mark Twain

The best thing about being famous is that it
makes it easier to get laid.
   Allen Ginsberg

HALF OF MANKIND IS DONE IN
BY ALCOHOL AND NICOTINE.
YET THE REST, ENJOYING NEITHER,
DOES NOT LIVE MUCH LONGER EITHER.
   *Lines in a Gasthaus, Oberndorf, near
   Salzburg, Austria*

If you're an asshole it doesn't matter whether
you are a white man, a red man, a black
man, a yellow man, a brown man, or a green
man. All assholes are the same color.
   *Navajo Guide, Grand Canyon (in
   conversation with Mike Harding)*

What Oscar Wilde and the court were contesting was not the evidence, but who had the right to interpret that evidence. It is no accident that the line 'the Love that dare not speak its name' haunted the trial, and has stayed with us ever since. It is not the love itself which was on trial, since even the law, since even our parents acknowledge that some men do have sex with other men. What was on trial was the right to speak (invent and articulate) the name of that love. The question was, and is, who speaks, and when, and for whom, and why.

Neil Bartlett, from Who Was That Man?

X

I can't make it any better than reality.
Hank Wangford (aka Dr. Sam Hutt)

I would like to be a beautiful male
prostitute — with a sting in my bottom.
Lord Byron

Art does not lie down on the bed that is
made for it; it runs away as soon as one says
its name; it loves to be incognito. Its best
moments are when it forgets what it is called.
Jean Dubuffet

I have always wanted to be a child and here I
am a lame old man — darn it!
Henry Darger

If you want to have clean ideas, change them
as often as your shirts.
Francis Picabia

The only tastes worth having are acquired
tastes.
Gilbert Adair

Dandyism is not fashion, or affectation or coquetry. It's the exact opposite. It is singularity pushed so far that it cannot be fully practised except by that supreme refusal which death means.

Jean Paul-Aron (first public personality in France to announce he had AIDS)

Never murder a man when he's busy committing suicide.

Woodrow Wilson

It was not my anger or my frustration that got in the way of my poetry but the fact that I viewed each anger and each frustration as unique — something to be converted into poetry as one would exchange foreign money. I learned this from the English Department (and from the English Department of the Spirit — that great quagmire that lurks at the bottom of us all) and it ruined ten years of my poetry.

Jack Spicer

The audience blew away — if there was an audience in the first place.

Edith Sitwell (speaking of Façade)

Every man in the world becomes beautiful when he's shooting his load.

The Reverend Boyd McDonald

In the *Puszta* (Great Plains) of Bugac, as the local saying goes, the breakfast consists of bread with bacon, the lunch is bacon with bread, and the dinner is a combination of the two.

George Lang, from The Cuisine of Hungary

Don't think — cook!

Ludwig Wittgenstein

The first movement begins as though it can't even count to three . . .

Gustav Mahler, on the Fourth Symphony

Yessir, going to stick with the youngsters —
keeps the mind active. And when these get
too old, I'm going to get some younger ones.

*Art Blakey, drummer, The Jazz Messengers,
at Birdland, 1954*

Poetry heals the wounds inflicted by reason.

Novalis

Journalism largely consists in saying 'Lord
Jones Dead' to people who never knew Lord
Jones was alive.

G. K. Chesterton

Where do I find all the time for not reading
so many books?

Karl Kraus

People say British food is terrible, but it's
not. It's wonderful. We set out to find the
wonder. We don't want green and red
peppers grown under glass in Holland and
packed in plastic containers. We want the
gnarled thing from our own garden.

Keith Floyd

What is a roofless cathedral compared to a well-built pie?

William Maginn

A statesman is a politician who has just died.

Ken Livingstone

The tourist in Ireland has only to ask and he will be directed to something; whether or not it is what he thinks he is looking for is another matter.

Ciarán Carson, from The Pocket Guide to Irish Traditional Music

Humanity does not change much; in some ways it even improves. Our international football games are occasions for violence, but football began in England with a severed head for a ball.

Anthony Burgess

Deprivation is for me what daffodils were for Wordsworth.

Philip Larkin

My talent is a horribly limited one. I want to
bless and (more often) I can only giggle . . .
My mind is not very fertile, and any success
I might have had is due to my own
shrewdness in not doing much.

Max Beerbohm

England is a horrible place with horrible
people, horrible food, horrible climate,
horrible class system, horrible cities and
horrible countryside (Gloucestershire is now
one big car park for Volvos with a few
scattered trees).

Stephen Pile, The Sunday Times

Good taste is as tiring as good company.

Francis Picabia

Adam passed water and thought nothing of
it. He defecated in a clump of leaves and had
no lawless sensations. Now voiding is ecstatic
and everyone perishes for the stroke of a
hand or a foot.

Edward Dahlberg, from The Sorrows of
Priapus

Mr. Rory McGurk, licensee of The Dehydrated Rambler, Boggerthwaite, knew that the bulk of his trade is done at weekends, when trendies from the towns regularly replenish his till without being able to detect the difference between a pint of good ale and the equivalent measure of weasel's urine.

> *David Bean, from Letter From Lakeland, in* The Guardian

Put up with me! I won't put up with you.
> *Aimé Cesaire*

Most of the trouble on this planet is caused by people who must be *right*.
> *William Burroughs*

Between ourselves, there are two things I have always observed to be in singular accord: super-celestial thoughts and subterranean conduct.
> *Montaigne*

Sitting here at my table I am beginning to feel like General Custer and there isn't an Indian in sight. Everybody over the age of 50 is a Custer. Nearly a third of the people in the framed photographs on the walls of this room are dead. And now I've run out of Perrier water.

Jeffrey Bernard

The behavior of the audience was highly creditable to Boston. There was smiling; there was giggling at times; there was applause. Nobody rose to remonstrate. Nothing was thrown at the orchestra. There was no perturbation of nature to show that Arnold Schoenberg's pieces were playing; the sun did not hasten its descent; there was no earthquake shock. It was as it should have been in Boston.

Philip Hale, Boston Herald, *1914*

He'd be better off shovelling snow . . .

Richard Strauss, on Arnold Schoenberg

I have often been more lonely than was
pleasant.

Arnold Schoenberg

Maybe we lost.

William Burroughs

Carl Ruggles, this sturdy American, is an
uncompromising foe of all the foibles and
follies of the old masters . . . He goes his own
way, sings his own shattered and acidulous
melodies . . . H.E. Krehbiel said of a certain
composition: 'It may be music in a hundred
years; it is not music now.' Perhaps that will
be the splendid future of *Men and Mountains*.

W. J. Henderson, New York Sun, *1936*

The tragedy of old age is not that we are old,
but that we are young.

Oscar Wilde

If Henry Miller often sounded like a village
idiot, it is because, like Whitman, he was the
rest of the village as well.

Gore Vidal

I don't feel that it is necessary to know
exactly what I am. The main interest in life
and work is to become someone else that you
were not in the beginning. If you knew when
you began a book what you would say at the
end, do you think that you would have the
courage to write it? What is true for writing
and for a love relationship is true also for life.
The game is worthwhile insofar as we don't
know what will be the end.

Michel Foucault, interviewed by Rux Martin

Some Friends think words I have used to
picture Hell unseemly, but Hell itself we all
know, and find it unseemly; yet it is as much
of God's making as Heaven. Good poetry
praises all His work. This is my small
contribution to His glory.

Basil Bunting, inscription in his long poem,
Briggflatts, *presented to Brigflatts Meeting
House, near Sedbergh, Cumbria (1977)*

One friend remarked that T. S. Eliot's clothes
were English, his underclothes American.

Peter Ackroyd

It would be completely wrong to say that they don't make Sam Whites, or journalists, like that any more. They didn't make them like that in the first place.

Frank Johnson, in The Spectator

We are moving from three-tier, class-based societies to two-tier, occupation-based societies. On top, the specialist, well-educated 10 to 15 per cent — us; below, the rest in a large, ill-educated mass, fed by the opiates of consumer-communications . . . At the very bottom, there may be a hardly-educated underclass who we would prefer not to recognize.

Richard Hoggart

It was the excitement of making a new best friend — the best, the purest feeling I've ever known.

Keith Hale, from Clicking Beat On the Brink of Nada

With a well-prepared anchovy sauce, one might eat an elephant.

Grimod de la Reynière

The Giant Man of Cerne stands out in chalk relief at Cerne Abbas in Dorset. He is nearly 2000 years old and represents the Celtic God of Hunting and Fertility, hence the huge club and 30-foot-long appendage.

Tea Towel, The Old Saddler Shop, Cerne Abbas

There is nothing wrong with cold soup. I believe leek, potato and cream is the Queen's favourite. But that, gazpacho and all manner of liquids employing watercress have no right to vanquish the hors d'oeuvres . . . All *Spectator* readers should give up soup for a year. Above all, no soup must be inflicted on guests (if you really can't do without, be like the French dogs and have a bowl for breakfast). Solid hors d'oeuvres only!

Digby Anderson, in The Spectator

Why do I paint? Actually, I know why I paint. It's because the world is so beautiful, and people are so moving. But this is not for publication.

Leon Kossoff

Happiness is rarely painted now. I become happy when my charcoal point shows the up-turning of a mouth or toes curling in happiness. The gargoyle's views of Francis Bacon allow no trace of paradise. The people I have drawn have been inspiring, beautiful, vital, elegant, innocent, desirable, patient, sensuous, and strong. I will always remember their generosity.

Jeffrey Camp

There are probably 'nice' people in every country—they are seldom met.

Basil Bunting

People today visit The Strange like they used to visit The Country.

Ian Hamilton Finlay

The stone that weighs 400 kilos can't be
moved.

Arab Proberb, quoted by Salvatore Scarpitta

Doctors again, operations again, nonsense
again, tests, inspections, inquisitions, visits of
publishers, scrutiny of lawyers, quarrels of
abbots, plagues of insects, bloody rain,
dragons in the woods behind the house, well
diggers pounding the earth, varmints
scampering, St. Elmo's Fire in abundance,
Northern Lights in the bedroom, incidences
of leprosy in the mind only—but leprosy . . .
Obviously, I haven't been anchoritic enough
these last weeks . . .

Thomas Merton, letter to JW, 1967

Weather here darkening. I am applicant for
social welfare, beseeching as well the
Luxembourg Embassy in Federal City to
inform me as just what salary or pension I
am to receive as Hereditary Grand Duke.
They have yet to reply.

John Wieners

Gave up smoking cigars in 1924; gave up chewing them in 1954.

Julian S. Myrick

Is there nothing to weep about in this world anymore?

Ben Shahn

I've tried my best to sell people on the idea that I can photograph anything that can be exposed to light.

Imogen Cunningham

It's like in posh places, you get to like avocado and spinach and other way-out foods. So you have them every time. You learn about wine and that's the scene for awhile. When you've done all that, then you can go back. You realize that the waiter's just there to ask you what you want, not what anyone expects you to want. So if you feel like cornflakes for lunch, you ask for them, without feeling like a northern comedian.

Paul McCartney

World's Who's Who says it proposes to list me as the author of *Briggflatts*, *Loquitur*, *The Spoils*, and *The Rise of the South African Reich*. I am thinking of adding *Papist Malignancy in Northern Ireland* and *A Child's Guide to the Cello*.

Basil Bunting

The thing about my painting is that it isn't painting anymore.

Willard Midgette

W. H. Auden
has gone to bed at nine o'clock
having been
unable to find his cock.

*David Hockney, table-talk, Odin's
Restaurant, 2–2-70*

Never mistake any rebuke of mine for mischief. Just ask yourself, what am I going to get out of rebuke to you? Hostility, rancour, spleen, a foe, what else is my guerdon in this flensed world?

Edward Dahlberg

About Tom Merton, there is no use speculating on how so much vitality is turned off so easily. Wisdom, I suppose, is the acceptance of Absurdity without becoming spooky or cruel. I am old enough now to have a fair collection of corpses.

Russell Edson, letter to JW

Forgive the pictures. They are a housewife's, a retired poet's, a mere dabbling in school kids' paints. A sudden fierce desire to paint everything I love — if it has simple lines and much color. But, it's likely, isn't it, that every poet feels a great desire to paint, no matter how primitively. You can write about a thing with great excitement akin to ecstasy, but paint, that takes love. Then too, it appeases my desire to possess things. But this, the desire to possess, has been leaving me anyhow. Marriage, however, brings with it the house, the kitchen stove, the living room furnishings, the land, a flower, the evergreen tree which Cid Corman suggests we should have to live on a little beyond us . . .

Lorine Niedecker, letter to JW, 1964

Ah, you say you were unable to locate the grave of Alfred Jarry. That is because, my friend, when he died, there was nothing left!

Dodo Conrad, in conversation, Paris, 1966

If it looks like a poem, it isn't a poem.

Joe Penner-Derrida

There are always more natives than ruins.

Earle Brown

Humor is the stud that keeps the collar from flying apart.

Joachim Ringelnatz

The expectation of life before death is as remote as the expectation of life after death.

Attributed to Ringelnatz

It's splendid to be a great writer, to put men into the frying pan of your imagination and make them pop like chestnuts.

Gustave Flaubert

Everything we meet is equally important and unimportant.

Thomas A. Clark

New Yorkers now see only what they want to see. The bodies don't bother them, they step around them.

Nicole Laurier

Thomas Gray walks as if he had fouled his small-clothes, and looks as if he smelt it.

Christopher Smart

Maybe I shouldn't say what I have is bad taste. Maybe I should say I'm devoid of taste.

Issey Miyake

I don't think the world at large realizes that we have a generation of kids who are nonconversant with *all* culture and *all* learning. Talk about the second volume of Spengler. This is it. The decline of the west has declined, and lies about like an old sock in a puddle, kaput, without any sign of life.

Guy Davenport

You were to invent a new world, but you weren't given any skills to do it.

Eric Fischl

Thanks for the article on Germany's current genius. Karl Heinz Stockhausen's Just Too Heterosexual for art. He eats pussy, affecting breath and *Tonkunst*. Pimples, prostate problems, giant stools, he's in the Beethoven line-up all right— music for real men. I like sissy art!

James Sellars

If you think you're boring your audience, go slower not faster.

Gustav Mahler

I keep casting loving looks at the gas oven. If only it were more up-to-date, poor dear, something with flashing chromium and deadwhite hardbake . . . as it is (dated about 1911, I should think) I haven't the heart.

Stevie Smith

If a man be gracious and courteous to strangers, it shows he is a citizen of the world, and that his heart is no island cut off from other lands.

Francis Bacon

Dear Sir, Your profession has, as usual, destroyed your brain.

George Bernard Shaw (to a journalist)

The one-eyed shed fewer tears.

Martial, translated by Laurie Duggan

Peter Langan, owner of the Brasserie in Stratton Street, Mayfair, reputedly told a woman who found a cockroach: 'Madam, it must have come from next door. That cockroach is dead. All ours are alive.' He is said to have eaten the insect, washing it down with a bottle of Bollinger champagne.

Owen Bowcott, in The Guardian

A poet who knows what it is he 'wants to say' may be sure it's been said already.

Hugh Kenner, from A Sinking Island

Always live in the ugliest house in the street, then you don't have to look at it.

David Hockney, on BBC Radio Four's Start the Week

I'm a throwback to remote ancestors. I really would look extraordinary if I wore coats and skirts. I would be followed for miles and people would doubt the existence of the Almighty.

Dame Edith Sitwell

The same tune is never the same tune twice.

Ciarán Carson

Children have to hate. It's unfair to assume they'll get on with each other. How can they? We aren't even as nice as puppies. We're just complicated, cannibalistic creatures.

Maurice Sendak

I am the shadow my words cast.

Octavio Paz

NAPOLEON: You, Sir, are a silk stocking full of shit.

TALLEYRAND: What a brilliant man to be so coarse.

God may forgive you but I never will.
   Dame Edith Sitwell, to Noel Coward

⊠ *About the Author*

JONATHAN WILLIAMS (aka Col. Williams, Big Enis, Lord Nose, Lord Stodge, Bent o' Dent, J. Jeeter Swampwater, et al.) is one of America's most outlandish and distinguished men of letters. He describes himself as a "poet, essayist, publisher, photographer, elitist, commonist, long distance hiker, and sorehead." He likes people who play all the notes, cover all the territory — and then double-clutch it. JW divides his year between a farm in the Blue Ridge near Highlands, North Carolina, and a seventeenth-century stone shepherd's cottage in Dentdale, Cumbria, England. *The Jargon Society*, the writer's press JW has directed since 1951, has published poets the calibre of Kenneth Patchen, Robert Duncan, Charles Olson, Louis Zukofsky, Robert Creeley, Mina Loy, Ian Hamilton Finlay, and Lorine Niedecker; and such photographers as Doris Ulmann, Art Sinsabaugh, Ralph Eugene Meatyard, Lyle Bongé, and John Menapace. It was the original publisher of Ernie Mickler's *White Trash Cooking* and its current wonderbook is ST. EOM IN THE LAND OF PASAQUAN. JW's current book under construction is *Walks to the Paradise Garden*, a collection of Southern visionary artists, outsiders, weirds, and wackos, with photographs by Roger Manley and Guy Mendes.